The Little Guide
for the
New ESL Teacher

Kathy Nosal

Misula Press
Orlando, FL

Printed in the United States of America

Cover photo credit: Unsplash.com.

First edition published 2017

10 9 8 7 6 5 4 3 2 1

Nosal, Kathy

The Little Guide for the New ESL Teacher / Kathy Nosal

p. cm.

ISBN-13: 978-0692812280

ISBN-10: 0692812288

Misula Press

"Any growth requires a temporary loss of security."

-Madeline Hunter

Table of Contents

Introduction 1

What To Do The First Day of Class 3

What to Do After the First Day of Class 17

What to do When the Activity Flops 27

How to Give Practical Feedback 29

How to Do a Mid-Course Check 33

What to Do on the Last Day of Class 37

How to Build a Learning Activity Portfolio 39

Conclusion 45

Worksheets and Activities W-1

Introduction

I was packed.

Highlighters, markers, paperclips, lined paper, unlined paper, sticky notes, pencils, pens, dictionary, and name tags.

I was ready.

Class roster, course text book, teacher notes, answer keys, password for the classroom computer, a bottle of water, cough drops.

And I was hoping beyond all hope that my lesson plan covered this first of 24, 2 ½ hour ESL classes.

The quote at the beginning of the book, "*Any growth requires a temporary loss of security*" describes how I felt. My TESOL certification program was terrific. I felt prepared to teach adult ESL. But, walking into my own classroom had me a little nervous. What was this really going to be like?

My first ESL course was a high beginning Reading and Writing class. The students were from several countries – Iran, Thailand, Saudi Arabia, Japan, Mexico, Germany, Brazil and Puerto Rico. They had diverse backgrounds – a restaurant manager, au pairs, retired college professor, housewives and stay at home mothers, an auto mechanic, a musician and an aspiring college student. To answer the above question, "*What was this really going to be like?*" It was positive, fun and hard work!

How This Book Can Help You

This book's purpose is to help you, the new ESL teacher, create a great learning experience for your students. We explore the rhythm to teaching a course – what to do the first day of class, at course mid-point and at the last class.

It will help you start building a learning activity portfolio. A portfolio collects your best learning activities for students and saves you lesson planning time.

This book walks you through what teaching an ESL course can look like. My experience is teaching beginning – low intermediate ESL students at a community college in the United States. This is the perspective I write from. Modify the ideas here for your students and situation.

As adults your students know how to do many things, they just do not know the English language.

You can help them.

Kathy Nosal
Orlando, FL
February 2017

Chapter 1

What To Do The First Day of Class

Your first ESL class. A case of the nerves is natural, or least I think so. I was nervous! Having a plan reduces anxiety, yours and your students, and results in a productive first class.

Walk into your classroom with a first day plan that works for you. If you are a detailed person, create a plan with lots of information. If you are a big picture person, then create a plan with the information you need, like a bullet list of what to do.

Here is what I have done for the first class in both a short and a detailed version. Use as you'd like –

First Day of Class – Short Version
- Before class
  · Write the day's agenda on the board
  · Make copies of handouts
  · Rearrange class desks/seating if needed
  · Have your class roster/attendance sheet out
  · Greet students as they come into the classroom
- Start class on time
  · Welcome the students and give a brief introduction of yourself
  · Review the day's agenda on the board
  · Review administrative items
- Assess students' skill (If your organization does not have a school sanctioned assessment, create your own. Ideas to follow.)
- Students fill out the *Tell Me About Yourself* worksheet
  · Students share their answers with the person sitting next to them
  · Students introduce their partner to the class

- Do the *What We Expect* activity
  · Working with a partner, students list what they expect of each other as students and what they expect of the teacher (you!)
  · Students share with entire class
- Review the course syllabus and course schedule
- Conduct a lesson
  · Create a short lesson so that the class "starts"
- Class close
  · Review what the students accomplished
  · Assign homework
  · Reiterate where to get the textbook, if needed

First Day of Class – Long Version

Before Class

Write the class agenda on the board (or project on a screen or give out as a handout).

EXAMPLE - AGENDA FOR THE FIRST DAY OF CLASS

- Class Welcome
- Assessment
- *Tell Me About Yourself* activity
- *What We Expect* activity
- Review Course Syllabus
- Review Course Schedule
- Lesson
- Class Close

Greet each person as they come into the classroom. Do not stay in front of the class or sit at your desk. Walk up to each student, introduce yourself and ask her name. Repeat her first name. Let her know she can correct you if you mispronounce it. A student may say that is does not matter if you mispronounce her name, but it does matter. It is her name. Many times I mispronounce a name on the first try. Do your best to say it correctly, she will appreciate your effort.

Class Welcome

Tell students about yourself but do not drone on. If you have an English-only policy in the classroom, mention it right up front. Then, go into administrative things like class meeting times, restroom locations, and emergency procedures.

Because English is the students' second language, I walk the emergency route out of the building with them. I quiz the students on this in the first few classes. In the middle of a class I will ask – *"If the fire alarm goes off while we are in class today, what do we do?"*

If your organization has an emergency text or email alert system, sign up for it.

I operate on the *if I know it I'll never have to use it* logic. As the teacher you are the leader in the classroom. In an emergency your students will look to you for direction. Given that, think about what you will do if there is an active shooter or a shelter-in-place situation. Take stock of what is in your classroom. If needed, what can you use to block the door from anyone entering the room? Is there a place to hide or escape? Think this through and then forget about it. (You do not need to share this with your class)

Assessment

This assessment information helps you for the rest of the course. Do this first so it gets done. If your organization does not have an assessment, here are some ideas. A suggested time limit is in parenthesis after each skill. Create an evaluation sheet to record each student's performance.

Assessment Ideas

Speaking Assessment (5 minutes for each student/pair)
- Listen to a two way conversation between two students
- In a one-on-one situation, show a picture and have the student describe to you what is in the picture. Have several pictures to mix up among the class.
- Have a one-on-one conversation with each student

Listening (20 minutes)

- Conduct a diction exercise. Read a short paragraph out loud 3 times. Students write down what they hear. Compare what the student wrote with the original paragraph.
- Play an audio clip (not a video) to do the same assessment

Reading Comprehension (30 minutes)

Give the students a paragraph or short story to read. Depending on the class level ask students to:

- Write one sentence about the story
- Write the main idea of the story
- Circle the topic sentence
- Write a summary of the story

Writing Skills (30 minutes)

Here are some writing topic ideas:

- List 5 things you do in your morning routine
- Describe your favorite place
- Describe the summer season in your native country
- Describe how to make a food you like to eat

Tell Me About Yourself Activity

It is important to get students active in the first class. This activity gets them talking with another person.

1. Handout the *Tell Me About Yourself* sheet, review and define terms as needed. Students complete the worksheet their own. See an example sheet after this description.

Optional: Pick 5-7 of the course objectives to gauge student interest areas. Rewrite the objectives into simple sentences and list them out. Have each student pick his three most important things to learn. This helps with lesson planning.

For example:

- I want to be able to talk about the weather
- I want to learn how to write using descriptions
- I want to get better at my listening skills

2. While students are completing *Tell Me About Yourself,* write on the board:

- *What is your partner's name?*
- *What is your partner's native country?*
- *How long has he or she been in the United States?*
- *What is his or her favorite color?*
- *What is his or her favorite food in the United States?*

3. After they complete their sheet, students share with a partner. Following the criteria on the board, each student will introduce their partner to the class.

4. You can model the introduction using yourself and one of the students. For example:
   This is Greta.
   She is from Germany.
   She has been in the United States for four months.
   Her favorite color is blue.
   Her favorite food is chocolate cake.

5. Keep the introductions loose and informal, students can stay in their seats and do this. The point is to get them talking, learn about each other and to break the ice.

6. After each introduction, say thank you to the student by name. Saying her name makes it personal, friendly and helps you learn names.

If you think sharing with the entire class is a big ask, then have each pair join up with another pair to do introductions in a small group. You walk around and listen.

EXAMPLE - TELL ME ABOUT YOURSELF
You may use a dictionary.

Name:_____

Month you were born:_____

1.Have you studied English before?   Yes   No

   If yes, did you study English in your home country? Yes No

   If yes, did you study English in the United States? Yes No

2. Do you want to improve your English for a job? Yes No

3. Where is your home country?

4. When did you come to the United States? How long have you

been in the US?

Please circle the three (3) most important things for you to work on in this class.

I want to be able to:

A. Understand the main idea when I read something in English.

B. Write a summary in English of something I read in English.

C. Talk with people about the news, weather and everyday things.

D. Correctly use verbs.

E. Learn more English words.

What We Expect Activity

Students discuss what they expect from each other and of the teacher. How do they want to be treated by fellow classmates? By you?

Does this seem like a weird activity to ask of students? I thought so too, but I learned that it is worth the time.

Asking students gives them ownership of the class from the start. The activity continues with them talking with each other. They express their thoughts and then agree on how they will treat each other.

1. Write on the board, side by side:

<u>What We Expect of Each Other</u>   <u>What We Expect of our Teacher</u>

2. In pairs, students discuss each item. Then they join up with another pair to share and discuss. As a group, they will share their expectations with the class.
3. Ask for volunteers to write their expectations on the board or to be a spokesperson for the group. Or, they can tell you and you write their ideas on the board. If you do this, use the language of the students and do minimal editing.
4. Take a picture of the board with your Smartphone so you can type up their expectations for the next class. Here is a sample from one of my classes.

> *Expectations of* each other:
> - To be friendly
> - To help each other
> - Not laugh at each other
> - To do our homework
>
> *Expectations of* the teacher:
> - To help us learn English
> - To correct us when we make mistakes
> - To be on time
> - To get to know us

Review Course Syllabus

Take time to review the syllabus in class. Don't just hand it out and have them read it later.

Here are some things to include on the syllabus if you do not have an organization sanctioned format:

- Course description and course objectives
- The criteria to pass the course
- The grading system
- The attendance policy
- The textbook requirement and other materials. If needed, explain how to get these materials. Have a date by when students must have the textbook.

If applicable, do a demo of online systems required for the course.

Explain to students that at times, even with a good attendance record and working hard, a person may not pass the class. This is not failure. It means a person needs to continue learning at that level before moving on. Some cultures will see this as failure so set the tone now that it is not. Be encouraging.

Review the Course Schedule

The schedule outlines the topics and work in each class. Make a note on the schedule that it can change depending on the needs of the class.

Some teachers add the homework and reading assignments on the schedule. I don't. I list the chapters covered during a class or week of classes on the schedule and assign the homework during each class. To me this is easier than having to change from the published schedule each week. Do what works for you.

EXAMPLE: COURSE SCHEDULE
Course Schedule
Low Intermediate Reading & Writing
(This schedule may change according to the needs of the class)

Week and Dates	Book Assignments	Due Dates/Tests
Week 1: February 8 & 10	*Getting Started Class Activities* Reading Book – Chapter 1	February 8 – Assessment
February 15, 2016 is the last day for a tuition refund. Please contact the Education office if you wish to receive a refund for this class.		
Class does not meet on Monday, February 15		
Week 2: February 17	Writing Book: Unit 1 Reading Book – Chapter 2	
Week 3: February 22 & 24	Writing Book – Unit 2 Reading Book – Chapter 3	
Week 4: February 29 &March 2	Writing Book – Unit 3 Reading book – Chapter 4	February 29 – Journal Due
Week 5: March 7 & 9	Writing book – Unit 4 Reading book – Chapter 5	March 9 – Mid-Term Exam
Week 6: March 14 & 16	Writing book – Unit 5 Reading book – Chapter 6	March 16: One-on-one mid-term conferences
Week 7: March 21 & 23	Writing book – Unit 6 Reading book – Chapter 7	March 21 – Journal Due
Week 8: March 28 & 30	Writing book – Unit 7 Reading book – Chapter 8	
Week 9: April 4 & 6	Writing book – Unit 8 Reading book – Chapter 9	April 4 – Journal Due
Week 10: April 11 & 13	Writing book – Unit 9 Reading book – Chapter 10	
Week 11: April 18 & 20	Writing book – Unit 10 Reading book – Chapter 11	April 18 – Journal Due
Week 12: April 25 & 27	Writing book – Unit 11 Reading book – Chapter 12	
Week 13: May 2 & 4	Review/Practice	
Week 14: May 9 & 11	Final Exam Review final exam; one-on-one conferences.	May 9: Final Exam May 11 – one-one-one conferences

Plan a Lesson

Plan a short lesson. For instance,

- Speaking or writing: Show a picture and ask the class to describe the picture. List the words used. You can ask them to identify adjectives, verbs and nouns. Or, ask them to create a story either by speaking or writing about the picture. If writing, have them do this on their own.
- Speaking: Have students work in small groups to create a round robin story. A round robin is where each person adds something to the previous information. Give a starting point, for instance:

    Elsa looked out the window...

    Students take turns adding to the story. This should be fun, creative, the point is to get them talking in English. They can go around 2-3 times to create an entire story. Walk around the room and listen, help as needed. Laughter is good, keep it light. Ask for volunteers to share (summarize) their story.

Class Close

As you end the class, congratulate the students on what they accomplished! Other things to mention at the close:

- Assign homework
- Review where to get the textbook
- State the next class day and time
- Ask if anyone has questions

Planning for the Next Class

Here is your homework for the next class:

- Type up the *What We Expect* answers. Do minimal editing. Make copies to distribute to each student and review them during the next class.
  Read and take to heart what they expect from you.
- Review the assessment information. Look for patterns and outliers. Patterns will help you shape upcoming lessons (i.e., most students could benefit from a verb tense review.) Outliers will give

you a heads up on possible skill level differences that are under or above the course skill level.

- Review the *Tell Me About Yourself* sheets. If you have students from many countries, tally up the results and share that at the open for the next class.
- Tally up the other information and use it in the *Who Are My Classmates?* activity sheet in the next class.
- Create the *Who Are My Classmates?* activity sheet. See an example on the next page. After the activity, review each box as entire class.

EXAMPLE: WHO ARE MY CLASSMATES?

Read each box and then find someone in the class who is a match. Write the person's name in the blank area in the box. Talk to your classmates to fill in all the boxes. Once you complete a box, find another person to complete another box. Continue until all the boxes have a person's name.

Find someone from Germany.	Find a person with a first name that begins with the letter I.	Find someone who is working as an Au Pair.	Find a person from France.
Find a person with a first name that begins with the letter Y.	Find someone with a first name that begins with the letter S.	Find a person from Iran.	Find a classmate who has children. How many children?
Find a classmate with a first name that begins with the letter D.	Find a classmate who works at a hospital.	Find a person who has been in the United States for more than 10 years.	Find a person who walks to class.
Find a person who was born in November.	Find a person who has been in the United States for less than one year.	Find someone who likes ice cream.	Find a person who has a pet.

Create Name Cards

Write the first name of each student on an index card. Use these cards to place students in pairs and small groups.

Before class place the name cards in the seat assignment for the day. Changing seats each class keeps cliques from forming. If you have an English-only policy, in a multi-native language class it keeps people who speak the same language from always sitting together.

You will see that students like the opportunity to meet and work with everyone in the class. This is particularly helpful for shy and quiet students.

Complete Administrative Responsibilities

Complete administrative information required by your organization. Be timely in turning in these items. Do not be the teacher they are always waiting on.

Create a Lesson Plan

It is a good idea to get a head start and always be a couple of lesson plans ahead of the course schedule.

Let's move on to the next chapter to talk about lesson planning.

Chapter 2

What to Do After the First Day of Class

Lesson Plans

At first I created detailed lesson plans with exact times for each activity. That did not work out when activities went over or under the planned time. I found using two broad time periods works better. For example, the first period is the start of class to the first break. During this first period the plan is to do the class open, a warm up activity, a skill activity and start the homework review. The second period is from the break to the end of class. The plan here is to finish the homework review, do a skill activity, practice pronunciation, and end with the class close.

As a new ESL teacher, walking into your class unprepared with the idea of *winging it* is a disservice to your students. They are adults. They will catch on. They expect you to come to class prepared. (Did they mention something like this in the *What We Expect* activity?)

The lesson plan is the roadmap for each class. With a lesson plan, when something changes you have a plan to change from. You won't be spinning in the wind.

See the next page for an example lesson plan format.

EXAMPLE – LESSON PLAN (2 ½ HOUR CLASS)

Lesson Plan #:
Collecting homework today? Y/N
Objectives:_____
_____
_____

Groups/Pairs in this class:

Activity/Materials/Book	Description	Time
Class Open/Attendance Announcements – 5		
Warm up activity – 15 Skill Practice/Lesson – 45 Break – 15 Skill Practice/Lesson 45 Homework Review – 20 Class Close – 5		

Lesson Activities

The lifeblood of a good course are relevant learning activities. They are the primary way to close the gap between what the students know and the course objectives.

As a new ESL teacher finding and creating meaningful activities for your students takes time. Even with a textbook, often there is something you need to change or add to meet the needs of your students. And, you will want to create additional activities. In the early days you will spend a lot of time creating your lesson plans. As you gain experience and build a portfolio of trusted learning activities, this time decreases.

After you create your lesson plan and activities, decide who is going to work together. Plan this out ahead of time; do not do this last minute in class. Class time can go quickly, so anything you plan and think through beforehand gives your students more learning time in class.

Pairs, Groups or Solo?

Think about what you are asking the students to do and then come up with the way you want them to work. Think through the makeup of your pairs and groups so that each student has the best chance for success at the activity.

Sometimes this means to group similar level students together, other times it will be to mix levels. Sometimes personality is important, place quiet people together and the more talkative together. When you have a competition activity, mix up the personalities.

Think – Pair – Share (work on your own – work with a partner – share with the class) is a good method. Another is to have people first work in pairs, then join another pair for the next step in the activity.

Get to know your students by walking around while they are doing activities. What is her approach when working with others? Does he dominate the conversation? This will help you form pairs and groups.

Color Cards

On index cards write color names - red, blue, orange, with a pen in the same color. (Use an orange marker to write the orange card).

To create a group, place name cards along with a color card to make a group. You can then say the orange team is working together, the blue team, etc. This saves time in class and students can see who they are working with in that class.

If you have a student with an engaging personality, have him work with everyone at some point. He brings out the best in others because he makes others comfortable. Also look for those who may be teachers at heart, at any English level. They can be great encouragers to less confident students.

Class Open

Always begin class on time, do not wait for everyone to be in class. This honors the people who are on time. That is not a judgment statement; people can be late for good reasons. But, if you always wait for everyone before you begin, then people learn to come late to class because *we never start on time.*

Warm Up Activities

After you finish the Class Open do a warm up activity. Another phrase for "warm up activity" is "activate learning." Keeping this second phrase in mind, then creating a good warm up activity is asking students to do something relevant to the day's class.

For example, if you are reading a book that takes place in the 1850's in America, then create an activity with that theme. Maybe find and play a game that was popular in the 1850's to give insight to that time period. Or, if your lesson is on stating opinions have an activity where students need to express their opinion. This can be simple, like *Opinion: Pizza is the best food* (and why) versus *Opinion: Pizza is the worst food* (and why).

Write the activity directions on the board, review them with the class. If you have late arriving students they learn to look at the board for the activity directions. This keeps you from repeating the directions for each late student, which is disruptive. The late student can read them and then you can ask if they have any questions.

In the first couple of classes, relevant activities are ones that help the students get to know each other. Here are some ideas:

- *Tell Me About Yourself* partner introductions (Chapter 1)
- *What We Expect* (Chapter 1)
- *Who Are My Classmates?* (Chapter 1)
- *Getting to Know You*: In pairs or small groups students interview each other. Use a topic that you are studying on that day. If the topic is food, create a list of interview questions like, *What is her favorite food? What is a special dish in her country? What is her favorite food or restaurant in America?* Ask for volunteers to share their interviews.

Skill Practice Activities

Evaluate activities by walking around, observing each student and noting results. During activities don't correct papers, sit at your desk, check your phone, or sit at the back of the class. Make yourself available to answer questions and to talk with your students. Walking around helps to assess students and assess the activity. You also get to see your students interact with other, work together and see their personalities.

For any activity, make note of what was effective and not effective. If the activity met its goal, consider adding it to your learning activity portfolio.

Here are some activity ideas grouped by skill. Change as you need.

Speaking Practice

- *Add to a story*: Pick a common topic like the weather, a topic from the lesson in the text book, or something from current events. Give the students a starting sentence and then one by one they add to the story. For instance, *"It was cold, but not as cold as yesterday."* This is good for small groups or to split the class in half.
- *Pose a question*: ESL textbooks have unit topics like weather, transportation, food and family. Say your lesson topic is School and Education. Have students answer the question *"Should schools have a grading system?"* You can start this as a pair activity and then move into groups. You can have like minded people together or mix it up. Discuss as an entire class.
- *Speak, write, and switch*: Typically in each textbook unit there is an aspect of grammar to cover. In this activity each pair discusses (speaks) and then writes sentences on the topic highlighting the grammar. Have them use the unit's vocabulary words.

For example, the unit topic is Nature and the unit grammar is adjectives. Have each pair write 3 sentences on Nature using 1 -2 adjectives in each sentence and a vocabulary word. They switch with another pair and find the adjectives in the other pair's writings. They discuss their answers (give peer feedback). Ask for volunteers to share with the class.

Listening Practice

- Have two paragraphs. Students work in pairs, each person gets a different paragraph. They take turns being a reader and a listener. The reader reads his paragraph out loud and the listener writes down what she hears. Compare to the original paragraph.
- Read a short paragraph to the class: First, read it slow, breaking up the sentences. Read it a second time, but speak a little quicker. The third time read each sentence in its entirety at a normal pace. Review as a class, or they can hand in their work to you for review.

Writing Practice Topic Ideas

- Describe your favorite place
- Describe your first day in America
- It is the year 2075, describe what the world is like
- What are the best/worst colors to use in advertising? Why?
- List the ingredients for your favorite recipe
- Write the recipe for your favorite dish
- Describe your daily routine
- Write about a favorite place
- Describe how you would teach someone your favorite hobby
- Is learning English difficult or easy? Why?

Give students the criteria that you are looking for in their writing, such as:

- Capitalize each sentence
- The paragraph must have at least five sentences
- Use at least three adjectives
- Write in the past tense
- Write a concluding sentence

Pronunciation Practice

Many times pronunciation questions come up during class. Students ask if they are saying a word or phrase correctly. To make pronunciation practice relevant, ask students for the words or phrases they want to practice. Here are some ideas to get that information.

- Hand out index cards or a piece of paper and ask students to write 1 - 5 words that they want to practice saying. Give 5 minutes to complete.

  Collect the cards and then during a break or when students are working on an activity, write each word on the board. Practice as a class. This is a nice way to end the class. It is productive, relevant and engaging for the students.

- Ask students for the sounds they want to practice. Often sh/ch and l/r come up as ones to practice. Go to the Internet and find some ESL pronunciation videos for those sounds. There are many. There are videos that show the correct mouth, lip, jaw, tongue placement when saying a word. Students find it helpful to see mouth placement for challenging sounds.

Practice pronunciation as an entire class. You say the word (or play the video) and the students repeat the word out loud. Even with a class of 20 people you can hear a mispronounced word.

Pronunciation frustrates some students. If you sense frustration, turn it around. Ask a student to say something like *"Today is a nice day"* or the word for *"holiday"* in their native language. Ask her to teach you how to say it. I do a terrible job of saying anything correctly in any language the first time, which makes the point. And brings a smile to the student. It was not easy for me because it is new for me while it is easy for her. Just be encouraging and let her know she can do it!

Students will also help each other with pronunciation, which is great! I like to see this and it builds confidence as they help each other.

Vocabulary Practice
Unless you are teaching a Vocabulary class, new vocabulary will be a part of the textbook units. Often it is the same activity in each unit. Here are some ideas to mix up vocabulary practice:

- *Guess a word* (Hotseat): Use words from the textbook unit. See *Hotseat* activity directions in the *Worksheet and Activities* section.
- *Draw a word*: Use words from the textbook unit. Do this in small groups or split the class in half. One student draws and the others guess the word. The drawing student remains silent.
- *Reading in context*: Students read a paragraph that is a level above them. Then, they guess the unknown words by the other words in the sentence. This is a good solo activity. Review in pairs and as a class.

Teach students how to create a vocabulary notebook. They hear and see a lot of new words outside of class, so this is a way they can learn on their own. See an example of a *Vocabulary Notebook* in the *Worksheets and Activities* section.

Students will ask you what a word means. It is easy to just answer the question. Instead, first ask if someone else knows what the word means.

Often another student will know. If no one does, then you can all look up the word together and then have a discussion about it. Help students get into the habit of looking up words on their own.

Reading Practice

Give out a short reading and a related a set of questions. Students read it on their own, then work in pairs or small groups to answer the questions. Assign each group a question to answer. Each group reports their assigned answer to the class. For instance,

- What is the main character doing? (Orange group)
- In one sentence, what is the story about? (Blue group)
- What is the topic sentence? (Green group)
- Is there a concluding sentence? What is it? (Red group)
- Do you agree or disagree with the article? Why? (Everyone)
- Circle the adjectives used in the story. (Everyone)

Here are websites with ESL reading materials of various levels:

- Voice of America, voa.org. At the homepage click on the Learn English tab.
- Breaking News English, breakingnewsenglish.com. Timely news articles written for various ESL levels. There is a 2 page worksheet for many of the articles.

A Note of Caution

There are a lot of free ESL resources on the Internet. Do be mindful of using materials designed for elementary school children. A worksheet concept may be helpful, but is the design for a 7 year old child? Your students do not need to learn the difference between the sun and rain. They need to learn to speak and write the words *sun* and *rain* in English.

Will the Activity Work?

The role of a teacher is to stretch her students. We don't want to embarrass them, but we do want to move them ahead. Sometimes stretch type activities feel like a gamble. I had an activity where the students, in groups of four, taught each other different paragraph types. It was near the end of the course; I felt like the students would find the activity agreeable but it was a stretch. But, you never know...Not only did they like the activity, they did great with it!

You just never know until you try.

Chapter 3

What to do When the Activity Flops

You planned. In fact it took you quite a bit of time to plan.

But it is not working. The great 40 minute activity is not only done in 10 minutes, but it went flat. Really flat. Oh, and you still have one hour left in class with about 15 minutes of planned activities.

You will have activity flops. It happens. It will happen. So help yourself and your students by always having back-up activities. (One of the benefits of creating a learning activity portfolio)

If an activity did not work and you're not sure why ask your students. Do keep in mind that in some cultures it may be improper to say something negative front of others. If this is the case, let students know they can speak with you after class.

Take time to address what they say. If it was too easy, then congratulate them on what they know! If they did not understand the activity, then apologize for not being clear. Do not let them think they messed up by not understanding.

Most of all don't beat yourself up. Learn from it, do not dwell on it. Let it go and move on.

Chapter 4

How to Give Practical Feedback

Giving feedback is a balancing act. At first you may feel compelled to correct many things – word order, pronunciation, word choice, and tense – all in one sentence! First focus on what you are currently teaching and correct that. If nothing on that front needs correction, then correct other items. Correct anything that could be embarrassing (i.e., unknowingly saying curse word.)

Students may think the ups and downs of learning equates to failure. They worry they aren't *getting it*. Say to students, *"You are learning English, when you learn anything you make mistakes. Just keep going!"*

In giving feedback, don't put perfection on your students. Be constructive. Help them communicate. Encourage. Correcting every little thing deflates people. Don't strive for perfection, strive for their excellence.

Native English speakers do not speak perfect English. Look at this conversation between Joe and Bob.

> Joe: *"I'm gonna go to the store."*
>
> Bob: *"When."*
>
> Joe: *"Dunno, 6 maybe. Want somethin'?"*
>
> Bob: *"Chips, milk. Here's 5."*
>
> Joe: *"K."*

The dialog communicates, you know what they mean, but it is by no means perfect English.

What is the End Result?

Give clear criteria at the beginning of an activity. Let students know what you are looking for, the end result. This allows for directed feedback. For example:

- *Pretend you are sitting on a park bench. Write what you see happening. You must write a paragraph with 5 – 7 sentences. Use the progressive present tense. Give your paragraph a title.*
- *Use the "Home Town Restaurant" menu and role play with your group ordering a meal from the menu. Each person takes a turn at ordering a meal and at taking the order.*
- *Complete the vocabulary worksheet on your own. Then, share your answers with your partner. Together, prepare to share some of your answers with the class.*

Writing Journals

If you are teaching writing, I recommend having the students work on a writing journal.

A writing journal is not a diary. Students can write about whatever they want and it helps builds their writing confidence. Writing journals are about conversing with the student, not correcting their writing. You have the opportunity to correct writing assignments where presumably they are making similar errors.

You do not have to collect journals every week. If you have a 10 week class you could collect the journals three times.

Give guidance for the amount of writing. For instance, you want to see four journal entries and each entry must have at least one and no more than three paragraphs.

Write comments on the content, for instance:

- *Thank you for sharing about your mother's garden in your home country.*
- *I didn't know you write music!*
- *I like to walk my dog in the morning too.*

Reading and commenting on the journals takes time, but you learn a lot about your students. You also see improvement in their writing skills.

Speaking Practice Suggestion

There are students that outside of the classroom speak minimal English. They spend most of their time with family and friends from their native country and do not need to speak it. The conundrum is that they do want to learn English but they don't seek practice. I do not like to tell someone how to run their home. But, I do make the suggestion that they take time each day to speak English with family or friends.

Peer Review and Feedback

You do not always have to be the one person to give students feedback. Let students give feedback to each other. This gives students a chance to help each other and lets them see what they know. Peer reviews are good pair work or in groups of three.

Create a peer review feedback form for students to use. A peer review form for writing could look like this:

- Does the paragraph have a title?
- Are there at least 5 sentences?
- Make changes to incorrect verb tense.
- Make changes to incorrect use pronouns.

EXAMPLE – PEER LISTENING AND FEEDBACK FORM

Listen to each group's presentation and write answers for each question. You will share what you write with the group.

What are the names of the people in this group?

What is the title of the topic?

What are the 3 important tips this group told us?

Did everyone in the group speak?

Teach students to check their own work. For a writing assignment, create a short checklist so they can self-edit their work. This helps them become independent. They hand in the checklist along with their writing assignment.

EXAMPLE - SELF EDIT CHECKLIST

Each sentence has a subject and verb. Yes / No / Not Sure

Capitalization and end punctuation is correct. Yes / No / Not Sure

I checked words in a dictionary for correct spelling. Yes / No

---

Chapter 5

How to Do a Mid-Course Check

Likely you will conduct a mid-term exam to assess your students' progress. To help students review for the exam, create a *Things to Think About* handout. Include the most common errors you see with the students. Tailor the handout to the students in the class.

Some organizations require a one-on-one mid-term conference with each student. This is a good thing. If your organization doesn't require these, I encourage you to do them.

One-on-one conferences provide individual time with each student. It gives each student a chance to let you know how they think the class is going. Use your student record and mid-term results as the foundation for each one-on-one. Take notes during each conversation.

Ask each student:

- How is the class helping you? Not helping you?
- What do you like about the class? Not like?
- What do you think you need to work on?
- How can I help you?

Share with students:

- What she is doing well
- Review her mid-term results, both problem areas and good areas
- Address any issues like poor attendance or low class participation. Talk about ways to improve.

If you are doing the conferences during a class, have the students work on a group project. The classroom noise provides some privacy for your conversations. To be fair to everyone, have a time limit for each one-on-one. Let the students know this before you begin and emphasize that it is to be fair. It allows you to politely stop a discussion if need be.

Between the one-on-ones check in with the class to see how the project is coming along and if they have questions.

Example - Mid-term Review: Things to Keep in Mind

Punctuation
Make sure punctuation at the end of a sentence is clear.
A period (.) goes at the end of a sentence.
A comma (,) is used in a sentence.

Capitalization
Make sure the first word in a sentence is capitalized. Make sure the letter is bigger than the letters in the rest of the word.

Verb tense
Keep reviewing the irregular past tense verb lists.

People or Person?
Person is singular. *A person saw the traffic accident and called the police.*
People is plural. *Many people were late for work because of the traffic accident.*

A or An?
Use 'a' before a word beginning with a consonant. (a cat, a desk)
Use 'an' before a word beginning with a vowel or a silent 'h' (example: an apple, an hour).

Past tense was/were
Use 'was' for singular. *I was going to the store.*
Use 'were' for plural. *They were going to the store.*

EXAMPLE: STUDENT RECORD WITH COURSE OBJECTIVES

Student Name:_____

1. Course Objective: Write a paragraph with a topic sentence and a concluding sentence.
Assignment: Write a paragraph about your favorite season.
Completed? Yes/No
Remarks:

2. Course Objective: Write a descriptive paragraph; the paragraph must be 5 – 7 sentences long.
Assignment: Write a descriptive paragraph on a topic of your choice.
Completed? Yes/No
Remarks:

3. Course Objective: Identify the main idea in a short article.
Assignment: Read the article, *"Blue Skies and Clear Water"*
Completed? Yes/No
Remarks:

:

Chapter 6

What to Do on the Last Day of Class

This chapter assumes you have the final exam results and final grades for the last class.

Giving Out Grades

Before you begin, mention to the class that not everyone is comfortable discussing their grade with other students. Ask them to not ask each other about grades while in the classroom. (Admit that you can't stop people from asking outside the classroom.) Also say that if a person does not want to share his grade it does not mean that he failed the class. Instead, he may believe it is private information. When I mention this several people always nod in agreement.

Make this a personal time. Use the same format as the one-on-one conferences at the course mid-point. Meet with each student and explain what went into their grade. Some will be happy, some will be disappointed. You may be surprised at a student's emotion, particularly if unhappy with her good grade. She thinks it's low. If so, ask questions to see why she is disappointed with her grade. Address her answers as best you can. You may not dispel her disappointment but you can listen to her.

Encourage all students to continue with their English and give them individual ideas on how to do that. For some it will be to take the next level course. For others it means they should re-take the current class.

It should not be a surprise to a student that he needs to re-take the course. Show by way of his student record and other examples why he did not pass the class. This is why it is good to have a mid-term conference and of course extra conferences as needed.

Make it Personal

If you are working with paper records, put together a packet for each student. It is a personal way to give them their course records, grades, final exam and other information. Create a cover sheet with the student's first name on it. Give each student her packet during the one-on-one.

Last Class Activity

While doing the one-on-ones choose an activity that is fun and/or interesting. Some ideas are:

- Do an activity that was well received during the course
- If you kept an early assignment, this is the time to have them redo the assignment and compare the two. They do the assignment and then you give them their previous work. For instance,
  - Students write on a previous topic and compare to their earlier same assignment
  - Reread an early reading comprehension assignment and have students answer the comprehension questions again. Compare previous answers.
  - Reshow a picture and ask the students to describe the picture again. Compare previous work.

Giving back an early assignment helps students see their improved English skills. It is encouraging for them to see this perspective. Or, if they have not progressed, it shows that too.

Course Close

Before this last class ends, remind students of anything they are responsible for at the end of the course. Do they need to hand in paperwork to the Education office? Give back an ID?

After the students leave, take a moment to write down your lessons learned. Write down your impressions, good and bad. What would you do and not do again? Look at these lessons learned as you plan your future ESL courses.

Oh, and by the way - Congratulations, you just taught your first ESL course!

Chapter 7

How to Build a Learning Activity Portfolio

Build a portfolio of trusted learning activities. This will help yourself and your students. It will house the best activities for your students and saves you lesson planning time. Create a portfolio folder on your computer and always be looking to add new activities to it.

Here are some activities to get you started. Activities previously mentioned in this book are included in this chapter so that all activities are in one place for you.

Jigsaw (Good for: Reading, Writing, Speaking, Listening)

Split the class into groups or pairs, each getting a part of a main topic. Each group becomes the expert on their part. You provide the article on the topic.

For example: You have a brochure on *How to Prepare for a Winter Snowstorm*. The brochure topics are:

- Preparing your home
- Getting supplies to shovel and move the snow
- Knowing the dangers of a winter storm
- What to do if you have an emergency

Cut up the brochure so each group only sees their topic. Each group reads their topic and prepares a presentation for the rest of the class. If they have Smartphones, let students use them for research. In a speaking class, create a *"What to Listen For"* peer review sheet. It should match the criteria you give students to prepare for their presentations. At the end of each presentation, each group reviews their feedback sheets. This provides feedback to students and gives students listening practice.

For a writing jigsaw, you can compile all the parts (not re-type) and then put them together and have copies for the next class. You can also ask for volunteers to do this.

A Jigsaw activity is good for a class project. I've used this during a one-on-one mini-conference class. The students were in four small groups. Each group had partial information on learning styles. The goal was to create a brochure for new Low Intermediate ESL students on learning styles and learning English. They first worked in small groups on their part, then with another group to review and provide feedback on their work. Then, they all came together to create the brochure. As a class they decided who would write the introduction, the summary, the titles and create the final format. They did this all handwritten, not with a computer.

Pair, Join Another Pair (Good for: Reading, Writing, Speaking, Listening)

Pair work is good because it lets students focus and learn together. But, small groups are good too! So, do both. Do Part 1 of the activity in pairs, and for Part 2 of the activity have pairs join another pair. This is a good way to review homework.

For instance, assign each group a part of the homework to report back to the rest of the class. Walk around during this activity so you can answer questions on where there is disagreement on answers. Disagreement is good. It helps students think through their answers and explain their reasoning, in English.

This format is good for students who get overwhelmed by doing everything as a whole class. Or, for those who like to think through things first before answering questions. Working first with one person and then in a small group of four helps build confidence and increase participation.

Pictures (Good for: Writing, Speaking, Vocabulary, Grammar)

Showing a picture is simple and creative. Have the students write about or tell a story about a picture.

Say you have a picture of a young boy and his dog:

- If you want to focus on vocabulary words, provide words for them to use in the activity. The words must relate to the picture (brown, spots, stick, boy, grass) Students match each word to its place in the picture.
- If you want to focus on grammar, you can ask students to use prepositions to describe the picture. (i.e., The dog is under the tree) Or to pick out adjectives or verbs or nouns. Have students work on their own or in pairs.
- As an individual assignment, students write a story about the picture. They can hand it in to you, or provide peer feedback. Provide criteria for them to use when reviewing a classmates writing. (But you'll want to read them to see their creativity!)

Role Plays

Consider the current teaching topic and make it real, bring it to life. With these activities begin by asking students what are some common words and phrases they have heard in these situations. Examples:

- If the topic is *Restaurants and Eating Out*, pick up some take-out menus at a local popular restaurant. Have students take turns ordering from the menu, taking the order and being the restaurant host. Common phrases are *"May I take your order?"*, *"What is the soup of the day?"*
- If the topic is *Shopping*, go to a big box store and pick up a bunch of sale flyers. Set up an activity where they take turns looking through the flyer and purchasing items. Common phrases are *"Do you have this in a smaller size?" "Would you like to pay cash or credit?"*

Role plays are flexible and easily tailored to student level.

Activities Mentioned Earlier in the Book

Speaking Practice
- *Add to a story*: Pick a common topic like the weather, a topic from the lesson in the text book, or something from current events. Give the students a starting sentence and then one by one they add to the story. For instance, *"It was cold, but not as cold as*

yesterday." This is good for small groups or to split the class in half.

- *Pose a question*: Say your lesson topic is School and Education. Have students answer the question *"Should schools have a grading system?"* You can start this as a pair activity and then move into groups. You can have like minded people together or mix it up. Discuss as an entire class.
- *Speak, write, and switch*: ESL textbooks have unit topics like weather, transportation, food or family. In each unit there is an aspect of grammar to cover. In this activity each pair discusses (speaks) and then writes sentences on the topic highlighting the grammar. Have them use the unit's vocabulary words. For example, the unit topic is Nature and the unit grammar is adjectives. Have each pair write 3 sentences on Nature using 1 -2 adjectives in each sentence and a vocabulary word. They switch with another pair and find the adjectives in the other pair's writings. They discuss their answers (give peer feedback) or you can have them share with the class. Ask for volunteers to share.

Listening Practice
- Read a short paragraph to the class: First, read it slow, breaking up the sentences. Read it a second time, but speak a little quicker. The third time read each sentence in its entirety at a normal pace. Review as a class, or they can hand in their work to you for review.

- Have two paragraphs. Students work in pairs, each person gets a different paragraph. They take turns being a reader and a listener. The reader reads his paragraph out loud and the listener writes down what she hears. Compare to the original paragraph.

Writing Practice Topic Ideas
- Describe your favorite place
- Describe your first day in America
- It is the year 2075, describe what the world is like
- What are the best/worst colors to use in advertising? Why?
- List the ingredients for your favorite recipe
- Write the recipe for your favorite dish
- Describe your daily routine
- Write about a favorite place

- Describe a favorite hobby
- How would you teach someone your favorite hobby
- Is learning English difficult or easy? Why?

Pronunciation Practice

Many times pronunciation questions come up during class. Students ask if they are saying a word or phrase correctly. To make pronunciation practice relevant, ask students for the words or phrases they want to practice. Here are some ideas to get that information.

- Hand out index cards or a piece of paper and ask students to write 1 - 5 words that they want to practice saying. Give 5 minutes to complete.

  Collect the cards and then during a break or when students are working on an activity, write each word on the board. Practice as a class. This is a nice way to end the class. It is productive, relevant and engaging for the students.

- Ask students for the sounds they want to practice. Often sh/ch and l/r come up as ones to practice. Go to the Internet and find some ESL pronunciation videos for those sounds. There are many. There are videos that show the correct mouth, lip, jaw, tongue placement when saying a word. Students find it helpful to see mouth placement for challenging sounds.

Vocabulary Practice

Unless you are teaching a Vocabulary class, new vocabulary will be a part of the textbook units. Often it is the same activity in each unit. Here are some ideas to mix up vocabulary practice:

- *Guess a word* (Hotseat): Use words from the textbook unit. See directions in the *Worksheet and Activities* section.
- *Draw a word* (think Pictionary): Use words from the textbook unit.
- *Reading in context*: Students read a paragraph that is a level above them. Then, they guess the unknown words by the other words in the sentence. This is a good solo activity. Review in pairs and as a class.

Reading Practice

Give out a short reading and a related a set of questions. Students read it on their own, then work in pairs or small groups to answer the questions. Assign each group a question to answer. Each group reports their assigned answer to the class. For instance,

- What is the main character doing? (Orange group)
- In one sentence, what is the story about? (Blue group)
- What is the topic sentence? (Green group)
- Is there a concluding sentence? What is it? (Red group)
- Do you agree or disagree with the article? Why? (Everyone)
- Circle the adjectives used in the story. (Everyone)

Conclusion

Her first writing assignment was two short sentences. For her last writing assignment Ana wrote several paragraphs. All were well written.

It seemed early on that if Ollie had his druthers, he would sit at the back of the class all the time. By the end of the course you would never have know that. He had the heart of a teacher and was such an encourager to all his fellow students.

Tia was in the United States for two weeks when she started the course. All the newness scared her. By the end of the course her speaking skills improved, and as important, she made a couple of friends in the class. None of them were from her native country.

Jose was a 70-something retired professor in his native country. He shared that he was writing his memoirs in his native language. Halfway through the course, his writing journal entries came from his memoirs. He translated them into English. There was such wisdom in this gentleman's writings; a joy to read.

Karina came to the United States 12 years ago. She had taken a couple of English classes but spoke her native language in her home and with friends from her native country. Her limited English was now an embarrassment to her high school age children. She was in class to change that. At first she was quiet and did not smile. At the end of the course she spoke with confidence. As a bonus, she blessed us with her pretty smile.

These student stories live out the quote, *"Any growth requires a temporary loss of security."* It was a joy to see them all grow!

It is an honor to teach adults English, and it is a humbling experience. Treasure it, and enjoy it.

Worksheets and Activities

Example - Course Schedule

(This schedule may change according to the needs of the class)

Week and Dates	Book Assignments	Due Dates/Tests
Week 1: February 8 & 10	*Getting Started Class Activities* Reading Book – Chapter 1	February 8 – Assessment
February 15, 2016 is the last day for a tuition refund. Please contact the Education office if you wish to receive a refund for this class.		
Class does not meet on Monday, February 15		
Week 2: February 17	Writing Book: Unit 1 Reading Book – Chapter 2	
Week 3: February 22 & 24	Writing Book – Unit 2 Reading Book – Chapter 3	
Week 4: February 29 & March 2	Writing Book – Unit 3 Reading book – Chapter 4	February 29 – Journal Due
Week 5: March 7 & 9	Writing book – Unit 4 Reading book – Chapter 5	March 9 – Mid-Term Exam
Week 6: March 14 & 16	Writing book – Unit 5 Reading book – Chapter 6	March 16: One-on-one mid-term mini- conferences
Week 7: March 21 & 23	Writing book – Unit 6 Reading book – Chapter 7	March 21 – Journal Due
Week 8: March 28 & 30	Writing book – Unit 7 Reading book – Chapter 8	
Week 9: April 4 & 6	Writing book – Unit 8 Reading book – Chapter 9	April 4 – Journal Due
Week 10: April 11 & 13	Writing book – Unit 9 Reading book – Chapter 10	
Week 11: April 18 & 20	Writing book – Unit 10 Reading book – Chapter 11	April 18 – Journal Due
Week 12: April 25 & 27	Writing book – Unit 11 Reading book – Chapter 12	
Week 13: May 2 & 4	Review/Practice	
Week 14: May 9 & 11	Final Exam Review final exam; one-on-one mini conferences.	May 9: Final Exam May 11 – one-one-one mini conferences

EXAMPLE - TELL ME ABOUT YOURSELF

Name:_____

Month you were born:_____

1. Have you studied English before?   Yes   No

If yes, did you study English in your home country? Yes No

If yes, did you study English in the United States? Yes No

2. Are you married?   Yes   No

3. Do you have children?   Yes   No

4. Do you want to improve your reading and writing for a job? Yes No

If yes, what do you do for work (or want to do for work)?

5. Where is your home country?

6. When did you come to the United States? How long have you been in the US?

Please circle the three (3) most important things for you.

I want to be able to:

1. Identify the main idea and some details when I read something in English.

2. Summarize in writing something I read in English.

3. Use a writing process.

4. Correctly use verbs.

5. Build my vocabulary.

GETTING TO KNOW YOUR PARTNER DIRECTIONS

Write these questions on the board or put up on a screen.

> *What is your partner's name?*
>
> *What is your partner's native country?*
>
> *How long has he or she been in the United States?*
>
> *What is his or her favorite color?*
>
> *What is his or her favorite food in the United States?*

To Students: Share your *Tell Me About Yourself* answers with your partner. Answer these questions so you can introduce your partner to the class.

To Teacher: Model an introduction with one of the students, something like this:

> *This is Greta*
>
> *She is from Germany*
>
> *She has been in the United States for four months.*
>
> *Her favorite color is blue*
>
> *Her favorite food is a cheeseburger.*

Thank each student and say their name after they do their introductions. This helps you and the student learn each other's names, and just makes it more personal and friendly.

WHAT YOU EXPECT ACTIVITY DIRECTIONS

On the board write:

How do we want to treat each other?

How do we want the teacher to treat us?

Take time to explain words if needed, make sure everyone understands the questions.

Have students work in pairs, and then join another pair to compare answers. Have one person from this group write their answers on the board.

Review as an entire class, combine where there are the same thoughts (get the class's permission - "Do these two things say the same thing or are they different?")

If you have a Smartphone, take a picture of the board and use that to type it up for the next class. Saves time and can review for complete accuracy.

Here is a sample of expectations from one of my classes.

Expectations of each other:
- To be friendly
- To help each other
- Not laugh at each other
- To do our homework

Expectations of the teacher
- To help us learn English
- To correct us
- To be on time
- To get to know us

EXAMPLE: WHO ARE MY CLASSMATES?

Read each box and then find someone in the class who is a match. Write the person's name in the blank area in the box. Talk to your classmates to fill in all the boxes. Once you complete a box, find another person to complete another box. Continue until all the boxes have a person's name.

Find someone from Germany.	Find a person with a first name that begins with the letter I.	Find someone who is working as an Au Pair.	Find a person from France.
Find a person with a first name that begins with the letter Y.	Find someone with a first name that begins with the letter S.	Find a person from Iran.	Find a classmate who has children. How many children?
Find a classmate with a first name that begins with the letter D.	Find a classmate who works at a hospital.	Find a person who has been in the United States for more than 10 years.	Find a person who walks to class.
Find a person who was born in November.	Find a person who has been in the United States for less than one year.	Find someone who likes ice cream.	Find a person who has a pet.

EXAMPLE – CLASS AGENDA (TO WRITE ON THE BOARD)

- Announcements

- Warm-up activity

- Skill activity

- Homework review

- Break

- Writing activity

- Vocabulary activity

- Class close

EXAMPLE – LESSON PLAN

Lesson Plan Day #:_____   Homework or Journal Turn In? Y/N

Topic/Objectives:_____

Groups/Pairs for this class:

Activity/Materials/Book	Description	Time
Class Open/Attendance Announcements	Announcements – writing journals due next class. Review the attendance policy.	
Warm-up – Whole class	Hotseat - Use verbs from Unit 3. Use both present and past tense. (Whole class)	
Skill Activity - solo	Write a descriptive paragraph using present and past tense. (Individual)	
Skill Activity – solo and then in pairs	Introduce future tense. Rewrite the previous paragraph using future tense (Individual and then pairs for peer review)	
Break		10:30
Review Homework - pairs	Unit 3, pgs 32-41	

Writing Time - solo	Topic - *It is the year 2050, what is the world like?*
	    -write 5-7 sentences
	    -use the future tense	

Class Close	Collect the writing time assignment, Homework- Unit 4 pgs 44-50.	

EXAMPLE: STUDENT RECORD WITH COURSE OBJECTIVES

Student Name:_____

1. Course Objective: Write a paragraph with a topic sentence and a concluding sentence.
Assignment: Write a paragraph about your favorite season.
Completed? Yes/No
Remarks:

2. Course Objective: Write a descriptive paragraph; the paragraph must be 5 – 7 sentences long.
Assignment: Write a descriptive paragraph on a topic of your choice.
Completed? Yes/No
Remarks:

3. Course Objective: Identify the main idea in a short article.
Assignment: Read the article, *"Blue Skies and Clear Water"*
Completed? Yes/No
Remarks:

EXAMPLE - MID-TERM REVIEW: THINGS TO KEEP IN MIND

Punctuation
- Make sure punctuation at the end of a sentence is clear. Press down on the paper with your pencil.
- A period (.) goes at the end of a sentence.
- A comma (,) is used in a sentence.

Capitalization
- Make sure the first word in a sentence is capitalized. Make sure the letter is bigger than the letters in the rest of the word.

Verb tense
- Keep reviewing the irregular past tense verb lists.

People or Person?
- Person is singular. *A person saw the traffic accident and called the police.*
- People is plural. *Many people were late for work because of the traffic accident.*

The word *because*
- Use when you are giving the reason for something.
- *Because of the traffic accident, many people were late for work.*

A or An?
- Use 'a' before a word beginning with a consonant.
- Use 'an' before a word beginning with a vowel or a silent 'h' (an apple, an hour).

Past tense was/were
- Use 'was' for singular. *I was late to class.*
- Use 'were' for plural. *They were late to class.*

LISTENING AND FEEDBACK FORM (PEER FEEDBACK)

Listen to each group's presentation. Write answers for each question. You will share what you write with the presenting group.

- What are the names of the people in this group?

- What is the title of the topic?

- What are 3 important tips this group told us?

- Did everyone in the group speak?

SELF EDIT CHECKLIST

Name:_____

Use this checklist to review your paragraph. Hand in this checklist with your paragraph.

1. Each sentence has a subject and verb. Yes / No / Not Sure

2. Capitalization and end punctuation is correct. Yes / No / Not Sure

3. I wrote 5 sentences. Yes / No

Topic #1 of 3: _____

Group #1: Becoming an Expert

You will be an expert on this topic so you can share with another group. Discuss the three most important ideas about your topic. Everyone in the group writes down these ideas in the box below.

Group #1– Topic:_____

Idea #1:
Idea #2:
Idea #3:

Group #2: Putting it all Together

You are now in a new group. Each person will share the 3 most important ideas from their Group #1. Take notes and write down the three most important ideas from the other two topics. After everyone has shared, discuss the topic and as a group write a summary of the reading. Be prepared to share your summary with the class.

Topic #1:	Topic #2:	Topic #3:
1.	1.	1.
2.	2.	2.
3.	3.	3.

Write a Summary here:

EXAMPLE - WEATHER VOCABULARY LIST WORKSHEET

Read the words in the first column. Then decide if you need to place a check under a column or columns for the word. Make sure to add words you do not know to your Vocabulary Notebook.

Word	This is the first time I have seen this word.	I know and use this word.	I need to learn this word. I will add it to my *Vocabulary Notebook*.
Example: *heat wave*	X		X
Example: hot		X	
warm			
cool			
cold			
sunny			
cloudy			
raining			
snowing			
windy			
foggy			

EXAMPLE: MAKING A VOCABULARY NOTEBOOK

Making a vocabulary notebook is a good way to learn new English words.

Here is what you do.

1. In a notebook, write a word you want to learn. These can be words you learn in class, hear a person say, or words you read in a book or online. They can be words you see or hear from anywhere!
2. In your notebook, you will make four boxes for each word.
3. In each box is you will write information about the word. .

Write the word you want to learn. *vacation*	Write the word in your language. *vacaciones*
Write the definition of the word. *A period of time devoted to rest, especially away from home.*	Write a sentence using the word, in English. *My favorite vacation was going to Disney World.*

EXAMPLE - HOTSEAT ACTIVITY (VOCABULARY PRACTICE)

Taking turns, a student goes up to the front of the classroom, facing the students and has her back to the whiteboard.

1. On the board behind her, write a word from the list.

    Example:

    Beach

2. To increase the difficulty, you can add words in parenthesis that students cannot say as guess words.

    Beach (ocean, sand)

3. The class calls out words to help the student guess the word. This should be interactive with lots of participation.

4. Don't let it get to the point where the guesser is embarrassed because she is not guessing the right word. Gently stop and help her guess.

Beach	Canyon
Listen to music	Cliffs
Write letters	Find directions
Make phone calls	Send text message
Lake	Desert
Cliffs	Hills
Snicker	Mountains
Hysterical	River
Coast	Wildlife

EXAMPLE - REWRITE A PARAGRAPH ACTIVITY

Directions: Rewrite this paragraph using descriptive words. Use the blank space to write.

My Neighbor

This is a story about my neighbor. His name is Mr. Taylor. He drives a car. When he drives his car many cars pass him. He drives from his house into town twice a week. He eats in town and goes to the park. I like my neighbor Mr. Taylor.

Write your paragraph here:

EXAMPLE - GROUP WRITING ACTIVITY WORKSHEET

Write your assigned part of the paragraph. This is the paragraph's topic sentence.

I am afraid of heights, so I never thought I'd jump out of an airplane.

Person 1: Beginning (where the main action begins, after the topic sentence)

_____

_____

_____

Person 2: Middle (where the main action or problem occurs)

_____

_____

_____

Person 3: End (gives the final action or result)

_____

_____

_____

After you finished writing your section, get together with your group members. Together, write transition sentences to make your paragraph flow. Be prepared to share with the class.

www.ingramcontent.com/pod-product-compliance
Lightning Source LLC
Chambersburg PA
CBHW060709030426
42337CB00017B/2816